50 GEMS

The Peak District

DENIS EARDLEY

AMBERLEY

This book is dedicated to my two grandsons, Aidan and Luke Roseblade

First published 2019

Amberley Publishing
The Hill, Stroud
Gloucestershire, GL5 4EP

www.amberley-books.com

Copyright © Denis Eardley, 2019

Map contains Ordnance Survey data © Crown copyright and database right [2019]

The right of Denis Eardley to be identified as the Author
of this work has been asserted in accordance with the
Copyrights, Designs and Patents Act 1988.

British Library Cataloguing in Publication Data.
A catalogue record for this book is available from the British Library.

ISBN 978 1 4456 8449 9 (paperback)
ISBN 978 1 4456 8450 5 (ebook)

Typesetting by Aura Technology and Software Services, India.

Printed in Great Britain.

Contents

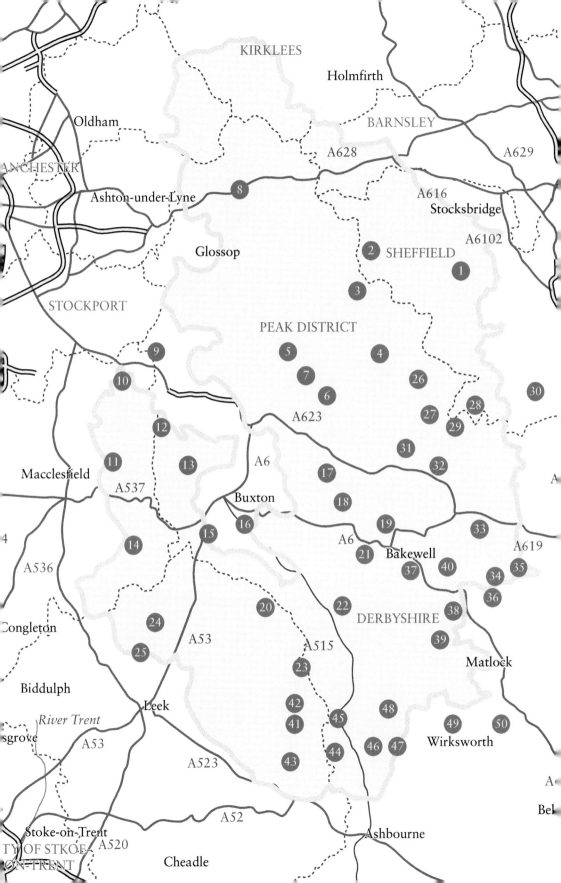

Introduction

There are fifteen national parks in the UK, which are independent bodies funded by central government. They are statutorily required to conserve and enhance the natural beauty, wildlife and cultural heritage of their areas as well as to promote opportunities for the public understanding and enjoyment of their special qualities.

The Peak District National Park was established in 1951 and was the first to be set up in Britain. It is stunningly beautiful and it is visited by people from all over the world. Nearly half the population of the country lives within 60 miles of its borders and it is highly accessible due to good road and rail communications.

Visitors come to the park to find peace, tranquility and adventure, with some of England's finest walking, cycling, climbing and caving readily available. There are nearly 200 square miles of open-access land for walkers to enjoy and 34 miles of family-friendly trails ideal for walkers, cyclists and horse riders.

The park, with its glorious ever-changing landscapes, enchanting villages, beautiful historic houses, famous attractions and hundreds of traditional events, attracts visitors time and again. Strikingly beautiful limestone valleys with magnificent clifftop views characterise the southern half of the Peak District, with the northern area featuring dramatic gritstone ridges and wild heather-covered moorland. The right to roam the privately owned northern moors was severely restricted until the 1950s. Now that access to roam has been negotiated, subject to certain bylaws, the moors are very popular with walkers. Here, the weather can change quite suddenly from bright sunshine to thick mist, making it impossible to find your way without a compass.

The Peak District National Park itself is home to approximately 38,000 people and, unsurprisingly, the local economy is heavily based on tourism and farming, with quarrying and manufacturing also playing a part. You will not find such a wide variety of outstanding landscapes, outdoor activities, traditional country events and great places to stay and eat all so close together and easy to reach anywhere else in the UK. The fifty gems in this book have been arranged in groups to enable the reader to explore at their own pace, by visiting just one at a time, or several. The fascinating historical information, legends and other stories will let both first-time and regular visitors to the Peak District take even greater pleasure out of their trips.

Northern Peak District

1. High and Low Bradfield (SK267925 and SK264920)

There are two parts of Bradfield conveniently named 'High' and 'Low', which accurately defines the two small settlements. Of contrasting appearance, they are set in the midst of glorious wild moorland scenery and deep green valleys. A steep drop of half a mile separates the two and both are only a short distance from north-west Sheffield, Europe's only city to have large parts of a national park within its boundaries.

Despite its close proximity to Sheffield, Loxley Valley has a surprisingly rural feel. The upper part of the valley is in Bradfield Dale, where a series of reservoirs sit snugly on the valley bottom. This, though, was not always the case, as on the night of 11 March 1864, between 11.30 p.m. and midnight, the Dale Dyke Embankment burst, causing what was known as the 'Great Sheffield Flood'. The torrent of water surged down the Loxley Valley, through Sheffield and even towards Rotherham.

It was the worst flood disaster in England in the nineteenth century. More than 240 people died, fifteen bridges were swept away and in only half an hour 4,500 homes were flooded lower down the valley. The damage was estimated at £0.5 million, a colossal sum in those days.

The Damflask Reservoir was built after the great flood and is the lowest in the cascade of reservoirs known as the 'Bradfield Scheme'.

High Bradfield is famed for its magnificent views, and none more so than from St Nicholas's Church, which celebrated its 900th anniversary in 2009. At the churchyard gates stands the Watch House, an oddly shaped building of Gothic design, which is now privately owned. It was built in 1745 to enable a lookout to be maintained for bodysnatchers who might wish to raid the churchyard. Payment was made at the time for corpses, which were used for research. Members of the family of the recently deceased kept watch from the building until natural decay rendered the corpses of no interest to the bodysnatchers.

To the west behind the church, up what is called Bailey Hill, at the edge of a wood, are traces of a motte-and-bailey castle. The attractive Old Horns Inn, like all the rest of the buildings at High Bradfield, fits perfectly into the picturesque scene too.

Above: High
Bradfield looking
towards the church.

Left: Cottages at
Low Bradfield.

Low Bradfield is a delight with its pretty cottages and Postcard Café and Stores. The most striking feature though is the Ibbotson Memorial Cricket Ground, with an accompanying bowls green and tennis courts. On the opposite side of the road is a large house named Burnside, which was the home of the Ibbotson family from 1865 to 1961. The Ibbotsons have lived in Bradfield for at least 400 years.

2. Derbyshire's Lake District (SK171898)

The Upper Derwent Valley is often referred to as the 'Lake District of the Peak'. It is surrounded by magnificent countryside where water and woodland, topped by high moors, predominate. In recent years forestry has become an important factor and the sides of the valley have been clothed in conifers. Not surprisingly, the area has become so popular that over 2 million people visit each year. At certain times the road up the valley beyond Fairholmes is closed to help protect the environment and a minibus service is operated. Disabled Badge holders are exempt from the road closure.

The valley was a very attractive location for the storage of water, with its long deep sides and narrow points for dam building. All this, combined with a high average rainfall, low population level and heavy demand for water from the industrial towns that surrounded the Peak District, made the case for reservoir construction. The Derwent Valley Water Board was set up in 1899 to supply water to Derby, Nottingham, Sheffield and Leicester, and the Howden and Derwent reservoirs were constructed.

At that time the demand for water was satisfied and although plans existed for further reservoirs, no more action was needed. Demand, though, continued to grow and the decision was taken to build one very large reservoir, to be called Ladybower.

Derwent Reservoir.

This entailed the flooding of the villages of Ashopton and Derwent and caused immense unrest. However, the project went ahead and the villagers were moved to new houses at Yorkshire Bridge.

Ashopton Viaduct was built to carry the Snake Road to Glossop and the Ladybower Viaduct to carry the road from Yorkshire Bridge to the A57.

The ancient Derwent packhorse bridge, which had a preservation order on it, was painstakingly moved stone by stone and rebuilt at Slippery Stones at the head of Howden Reservoir. The graves in the churchyard were excavated and the bodies reburied at Bamford.

A few properties built on slightly higher land survived, including the Shooting Lodge and former Roman Catholic School. Although the majority were demolished and flooded, the church spire was left eerily poking out above the reservoir when the water level was low, until it was blown up in 1947. The flooding having been completed, the opening ceremony was carried out on 25 September 1945 by George VI. In order to mark the occasion a commemorative monument was built close to the dam wall.

One person though refused to move, Miss A. Cotterill of Gwinnett House. She remained there until she died in 1990, at the age of ninety-nine, the waters of the

Ladybower Viaduct.

Above: View across Ladybower from the dam wall.

Below: Gwinnett House, Ladybower.

reservoir lapping at the front garden steps. You can easily pick out the house at the side of Ladybower when crossing the discretionary path across the dam wall.

Food is available at the refreshment kiosk at Fairholmes, Yorkshire Bridge Inn and Ladybower Inn.

3. Birchinlee, 'Tin Town' (SK165916)

The building of the Derwent and Howden dams in the Upper Derwent Valley brought an army of construction workers and their families into the area. To house the newcomers the Derwent Water Board built a model village, Birchinlee, off the A57 near Fairholmes Visitor Centre between 1902 and 1916. The population eventually rose to well in excess of 900 people.

Known locally as 'Tin Town', the accommodation consisted of workmen's huts, foremen's huts and married workmen's huts. The latter were decorated to a high standard. Facilities included a hospital, school, pub, post office, shops, recreation hall, public bathhouse, police station, railway station and even a rubbish dump with an incinerator. The work was hard, but that was compensated by the excellent living conditions and wonderful scenery.

When the Derwent and Howden dams were built, a railway line was specially constructed to carry stone from the sidings at Bamford to Fairholmes. In the 1930s, when Ladybower was built, the line was reopened as a timberline. When it no longer served any useful purpose it was purchased by the Peak District National Park Authority and is now a bridleway and footpath known as the Thornhill Trail.

Above: Fairholmes Visitor Centre, Ladybower.

Right: A former Birchinlee dwelling that has been moved to Hope.

Many of the families stayed on when the work was completed and made the village of Hope their home. Along Edale Road, opposite the farm shop, is probably the last surviving building to have come from the temporary village of Birchinlee.

A few remnants of the former village still remain and can still be seen on a delightful woodland walk to the west of Derwent Reservoir. A call at Fairholmes Visitor Centre to obtain a walk map is maybe the best option if you are a little uncertain of your bearings.

4. Yorkshire Bridge (SK201850)

The tiny village of Yorkshire Bridge, in the Upper Derwent Valley, lies in the shadow of the dam wall of the Ladybower Reservoir. Its neat, regimented rows of houses were built to rehome the inhabitants of the former villages of Ashopton and Derwent, both villages and the surrounding land having been submerged when the reservoir was completed and filled with water.

Yorkshire Bridge has its own pub of the same name. It dates back to at least 1826 and takes its name from an old packhorse bridge, which was the last crossing point on the River Derwent before the Yorkshire border.

Despite all the references to Yorkshire, you are still in Derbyshire; the boundary between the two counties is more than 2 miles away to the north-east. The visitor centre at Fairholmes, situated further north below the wall of Derwent Dam, tells the story of the 'drowned villages' and the birth of Yorkshire Bridge. It is a great place to visit, either for a walk in the glorious countryside that surrounds or to relax and have a picnic.

Perhaps the best-known inhabitant to have lived at Yorkshire Bridge was a sheepdog named Tip. Her master, Tagg, was a well-known local sheep farmer who helped found Hope Valley Sheepdog Trials, and during his later years lived at Yorkshire Bridge. He won a succession of prizes throughout the country with his sheepdogs and even sold one to an American for £1,000, a lot of money in those days.

On 12 December 1953, Tagg, aged eighty-five, went out for the last time with his faithful border collie, Tip, and vanished completely. Despite an exhaustive search, neither he, nor his dog, could be found. It was not until fifteen weeks later that Tagg's remains were discovered by chance, with the faithful Tip now completely exhausted lying around 5 yards away. Somehow, Tip had managed to survive heavy

Yorkshire Bridge.

IN
COMMEMORATION OF
THE DEVOTION OF
TIP.
THE SHEEPDOG WHICH STAYED
BY THE BODY OF HER DEAD
MASTER, MR. JOSEPH TAGG,
ON THE HOWDEN MOORS FOR
FIFTEEN WEEKS FROM 12TH
DECEMBER 1953 TO 27TH
MARCH 1954.

ERECTED BY PUBLIC
SUBSCRIPTION

Tip's memorial at
Derwent Reservoir.

snow, biting winds and freezing temperatures on one of the most hostile stretches
of moorland in the country. Tip was carried back to the rescuer's lorry and later
transferred to a caring home, where she was nursed back to health. Once the story
became known, Tip became famous not only in this country but abroad as well.
A year later, in May 1955 she died. However, the hearts of those who had heard
the story were so greatly touched that a memorial was erected at the western end of
Derwent Dam, in memory of Tip.

5. The Nag's Head, Edale – Start of the Pennine Way (SK122859)

Edale is a pretty village, but its stunning location is what attracts visitors in their
thousands all summer and at the weekends in winter. For many years, the Vale of
Edale had remained isolated. Its position, surrounded by the glowering heights of
Kinder Scout to the north, and a long ridge of hills to the south, made it difficult to
reach. However, everything began to change when the railway arrived in the heart of
the countryside linking Manchester and Sheffield.

For those who travel by road there is a large pay and display car park near the Village
Hall a short walk from the village. Car parking in the village centre is impossible.

The right to roam the privately owned moor above Edale was severely restricted
until the 1950s. Now that access to roam has been negotiated, subject to certain
bylaws, the moors are very popular with walkers. Kinder Scout, however, a plateau
that covers 5 square miles and rises to a maximum of 2,088 feet, can be a very
dangerous place. The weather can change quite suddenly from bright sunshine to
thick mist, making it impossible to find your way without a compass, but for those
who prefer more gentle exercise, the Vale of Edale offers a splendid alternative.

Above: Cottages at Edale.

Left: Nag's Head, Edale.

Tom Stephenson's classic long-distance walk, the 'Pennine Way' has its official starting point at the Old Nag's Head, built in 1577, in the centre of Edale. It follows the Pennine Chain for over 250 miles northwards to the Scottish border at Kirk Yetholm. Attracting some 10,000 walkers each year, it is a good test even for the most experienced walker. On the wall in the pub is a blank framed certificate, similar to that presented to those who complete the walk.

6. Peveril Castle, Castleton (SK149827)

Castleton is a delightful village that invites exploration with its cluster of old stone cottages. A sparkling little stream leads you from the centre to Peak Cavern, passing through the oldest part of the village. Along the main street are a large variety of gift shops, cafés and restaurants to suit all tastes.

Towering above Castleton is Peveril Castle, built by William Peverel, whose name is spelt slightly differently to that of the castle. He was a favourite knight of William the Conqueror, who made him bailiff of the royal manors in north-western Derbyshire.

At that time the Peak Forest was rich in both game and minerals and the castle was ideal for protecting both. Henry II built the stone keep almost 100 years later in 1176. It still stands today and can be viewed at close quarters by those people prepared to climb the steep zigzag path leading up to the castle, made famous by Sir Walter Scott in his novel *Peveril of the Peak*.

The castle is mentioned in the Domesday Book and is a Grade I listed building in the care of English Heritage. It has been described by Nicholas Pevsner as 'perhaps the finest medieval landmark of the Peak District'. Pevsner wrote a series of forty-six volumes of county guides under the title of *The Buildings of England* (1951–74).

The path leading up to Peak Cavern, Castleton.

Above: Main Street,
Castleton.

Left: Peveril Castle,
Castleton.

After enjoying the displays at the visitor centre a climb up to explore the castle remains and enjoy the superb views is likely to prove the highlight of a family day out. The children will be particularly amused when exploring the garderobe (medieval lavatory) to see it is open at the bottom and directly above the path up Cave Dale. It may not have been so amusing for the passersby when the castle was inhabited.

7. Winnats Pass, Castleton (SK135825)

Frequently referred to as 'the Gem of the Peak', Castleton is one of Britain's most appealing villages, set in a magnificent location with wonderful views in all directions.

Approaching from the south-west you descend into Castleton through the spectacular Winnats Pass with its forbidding appearance. The name is a corruption of 'Wind Gates'. It is in a limestone valley that was once under a tropical sea and as a result, the limestone is full of fossils of sea creatures, which lived here over 350 million years ago. The pass is classified as a Site of Special Scientific Interest (SSSI) and is one of the Peak District's most cherished possessions.

Winnats Pass.

Speedwell Cavern at the foot of Winnats Pass.

In the 1970s a number of landslips on the A625 opened a series of deep crevices at the foot of Mam Tor. It is appropriately known as the 'Shivering Mountain' because the layers of soft shale between harder beds of gritstone frequently crumble to cause landslips and temporary road closures. As Mam Tor lacked stability and would not stop shivering and sending down rockfalls, the momentous decision was finally made to permanently close the road and use Winnats Pass as the main road into Castleton from the west. Before this, the pass had been closed to traffic at the weekends in the summer to protect its grass verges.

In 1758, it was the scene of the horrific murder by five lead miners of a young couple journeying to Peak Forest to get married. The crime was not solved until the last surviving miner confessed on his lingering deathbed. It was later revealed the other four miners involved had also met terrible ends.

8. Longdendale Trail (SK078991)

The Longdendale Trail, in the far north-west corner of Derbyshire, is situated in an Area of Outstanding Natural Beauty. It stretches from Hadfield in the south to the Woodhead Tunnel in the north, along a wide well-surfaced track and is best approached along the B6105. The Trans Pennine Trail, part of an international

Longdendale Trail.

walking route that stretches through Europe, from Liverpool to Istanbul, also utilises a section of the trail.

The trail runs along a disused railway line, which is now used by walkers, cyclists and horse riders and runs parallel with the reservoirs in the valley. The chain of reservoirs supply water to the growing population of Manchester and Salford, and was constructed in the nineteenth century by damming the River Etherow. Originally, there were seven reservoirs, but Hollingworth Reservoir was abandoned in 1990 and has become part of the Swallows Wood nature reserve.

Here the Pennine country is at its wildest on either side of the valley. Much of the heather-covered moorland is access land over which people are allowed to roam the great moorland wildernesses of Bleaklow and Saddleworth Moor. There is much difficult terrain, where experienced walkers and climbers often come to test themselves.

The Longdendale Trail offers a much easier walk and is surrounded by superb scenery. There is a short but very rewarding circular walk round Torside Reservoir, starting from a large roadside car park off the B6105. On the northern side of the reservoirs, the busy A628, carrying convoys of lorries across the Pennines, contrasts sharply with the peace and quiet of the valley along the Longdendale Trail.

Fans of the cult BBC TV comedy series, *The League of Gentlemen* will know that Hadfield, just to the south of the trail, is the real Royston Vasey and will want to fit in a visit.

View over Longdendale Valley.

9. Torrs Riverside Park, New Mills (SK001852)

Spectacular New Mills! A lot of people who drive through the town by car, along the A6015, are completely unaware of the secret beauty that lies below and will dismiss my comments as an exaggeration. However, they are likely to change their minds after visiting Torrs Riverside Park, which provides access to an impressive gorge and an area of dramatic natural beauty.

Following massive reclamation work, the 'Park under the town' has taken over land left derelict by industry and now extends for 2 miles along the Goyt Valley. Trees have been planted, ponds created and easy access paths have been formed.

At the time the Industrial Revolution swept the country, the Torrs was an ideal place for spinning and weaving driven by waterpower. Set in a natural gorge, New Mills had the joint waterpower of the rivers Sett and Goyt. Rocky waterfalls and cascades allowed the construction of weirs to provide a controlled supply of water. The ledges along the riverbank, above the floodwater level, were ideal to build on. The sandstone rocks at the side of the gorge meant the builders did not have to go far for their materials.

The main problem for the mills set in the gorge was accessibility, with narrow steep roads that put it at a disadvantage when steam power started to replace water.

Above: Union Bridge, New Mills.

Below: Millennium Bridge, New Mills.

The next generation of mills was built on high ground on the other side of the gorge at Newtown, alongside the Peak Forest Canal and close to the railway station, which is still operational.

In 1884, the problem of access between New Mills and Newtown, on opposite sides of the gorge, was solved with the building of the mighty Union Road Bridge, one of the highest road bridges in this part of the country. Despite this, it hardly seems as if you are crossing a bridge, because the high parapets hide the view of the gorge.

One of the best of the many good viewpoints of the Riverside Park is from the platform outside the Heritage Centre. The centre, housed in a converted stone building, contains a finely detailed model of the town in 1884 when the Union Road Bridge was nearing completion. It is an ideal starting point for a visit to the valley below.

Only a short distance down the steps from the Heritage Centre is the Torrs Millennium Walkway. Derbyshire County Council's in-house engineers, not specialist bridge designers as might have been expected, constructed it. The walkway spans the otherwise inaccessible cliff wall above the River Goyt – part on stilts rising from the riverbed and partly cantilevered off the railway retaining wall, high up among a canopy of trees. It provides the final link in the 225-mile-long Midshires Way and is most definitely worth making a special visit to New Mills to see and use.

10. Lyme Park (SK965825)

Lyme Park is located on the north-west edge of the Peak District, off the A6, and offers a fantastic day out for all the family. Children particularly will enjoy themselves in the Crow Wood Playscape with its giant slide, tree house and rope walks.

In 1996, Lyme Park was used as a location for the BBC adaptation of *Pride and Prejudice*, starring Colin Firth. More recently it has featured in scenes from the chilling supernatural thriller *The Awakening*.

The park was originally the site of a hunting lodge, until in Tudor times a house was built there. It was the home of the Legh family from 1388 and remained in their possession until 1946 when it was given to the National Trust.

The house was transformed by the Venetian architect Leoni into a fine Italianate palace. Some of the Elizabethan interior still survives and contrasts markedly with the later additions in the eighteenth and nineteenth centuries. The staterooms are adorned with beautiful Mortlake tapestries, with Grinling Gibbons intricate wood carvings in the dining room. The large collection of unique English clocks is also of particular interest to visitors.

The 19-acre Victorian garden, with its impressive flower beds and appealing rose garden, together with the Wyatt conservatory are a delight, surrounded by a medieval deer park, with miles of walks across moorland and through woodlands.

A visit to Lyme though is not complete without a stroll up to the Cage, a Grade II listed building that is sited on the crest of a hill, from where you will be able to see for miles across Greater Manchester and Cheshire. The Cage was built as a hunting lodge and later used as a lockup for poachers. It has been restored in recent years.

Above: Lakeside view of Lyme Hall.

Below: The Cage at Lyme Park provides wide-ranging views.

Western Peak District

11. Pott Shrigley (SK945792)

The picturesque Cheshire village of Pott Shrigley is located on the western border of the Peak District, around a mile north from the small town of Bollington. The houses in the centre of the village huddle together close to the top end of two valleys, with Holme and Nab woods rising up to the rear. There are beautiful trees and fields with flocks of sheep grazing in all directions, giving the village a distinct rural identity.

Pott Shrigley has a long and interesting history, which for many years revolved around Shrigley Hall and its estate, farming and, later, mineral extraction. Originally built in the fourteenth century by the Downes family, who lived there for 500 years, it was rebuilt on a grander scale in the early nineteenth century by William Turner. In the 1950s it was sold to the Salesians as a Catholic Education Centre and sold again in the 1980s when it was converted into a hotel, which it remains today.

St Christopher's Church is a Grade I listed building, which is thought to have been founded in the late fourteenth century and completed in its present form by the building of the Downes Chantry Chapel by Geoffrey Downes in the late fifteenth century. Inside the church there is a fine fifteenth-century barrel roof and an oak

Cottage at Pott Shrigley.

Above: St Christopher's Church, Pott Shrigley.

Right: Pott Shrigley Cricket Club.

altar table that dates back to 1698. The oak box pews were acquired from St James's Church, Gawsworth, in the nineteenth century. Another building in the village with an ancient history is the Church of England Primary School, which was founded in 1492.

In the spring, the bluebells along the road up the hill towards Shrigley Hall are an impressive sight and attract large numbers of visitors. The village cricket ground is in a stunning location, which according to the locals, is one of the most beautiful settings in the world.

12. Jenkin Chapel (Church of St John the Baptist), Saltersford (SK989777)

Jenkin Chapel is in an isolated location at Saltersford, on the western side of the Peak District at the junction of three ancient trackways. These trackways were known as Salters' Ways as they were once used by packhorses carrying salt. At a later date, they were used by cattle drovers and sheep dealers.

The chapel can be approached from several directions and is not easy to find without a map. The route that I use rises up from the Goyt Valley, along an old Roman road known as The Street to Pym's Chair, before dropping down to the chapel. However, from whatever direction you come, the chapel is likely to remain in your memory much longer than other more conventional buildings, both for its appearance and scenic setting.

The chapel's outward appearance is more like that of a Georgian farmhouse with a chimneystack than for the purpose for which it was intended. The tower has an external staircase and inside the chapel are box pews, an octagonal pulpit and a carved reading desk.

It was built in 1733 by local people using local materials. They also raised the money to pay for a minister and added a tower twenty-two years later. It is an Anglican chapel in the diocese of Chester and services are still held there on the second and fourth Sundays between Easter and Christmas. At the Harvest Festival in September, the churchyard is occupied by a large congregation for an open-air service – weather permitting.

There is disagreement about the origin of the chapel's name. One theory is that it is named after a man called Jenkin from North Wales who traded at the crossing, and weight is added to this argument as the track marking stone at this junction was known as 'Jenkin Cross'. Another theory is that it is named after a 'fiery Welsh preacher' who preached at the horse fairs held at the crossing.

Jenkin Chapel, Saltersford.

13. Goyt Valley (SK014758)

The Goyt Valley is off the A537 Buxton to Macclesfield road, where you follow the sign to a small car park at Derbyshire Bridge, but beware from this point traffic is one way only and in the other direction. Alternatively, the valley can be approached off the A5004 Buxton to Whaley Bridge road.

The ruggedly picturesque Goyt Valley, surrounded by heather-clad moors, has been a popular place for visitors since Victorian times. It was the home to Neolithic farmers around 3000 BC, who were the first to start felling trees and clearing the ground for cultivation. The appearance of the valley changed dramatically in the 1930s when the Fernilee Reservoir was built and, some thirty years later, the Errwood Reservoir. Now the reservoirs provide leisure facilities, in a valley rich in industrial heritage and wildlife.

Much of this glorious landscape is open and accessible to walkers and is crisscrossed by a maze of excellent well-signposted public footpaths. Most of the moorland has been designated a Site of Special Scientific Interest to help protect the habitat and its valued wildlife.

The valley was predominantly used for farming for many centuries. Surprisingly, considering its location, in more recent years it has been the home of several thriving industries. Goyt's Moss Colliery, sited near Derbyshire Bridge, was quite extensive and it was from Goytsclough Quarry that Thomas Pickford set up a family business mending roads. The business progressed to such an extent that by the eighteenth century James Pickford was known as the 'London to Manchester Waggoner'. Today the company still thrives as one of the major removal and storage businesses in Europe. There were also several other quarries in the valley, coal-mining shafts, a paint mill and a gunpowder factory.

It is thought the factory may date back to the sixteenth century and have supplied the ammunition for Sir Francis Drake to fight the Spanish Armada. The factory was positioned where the Fernilee Reservoir is now to be found. At the time a network of

Fernilee and Goyt Boat Club.

Goyt Bridge.

Ruins of
Errwood Hall,
Goyt Valley.

tramways and a narrow canal were used to transport the explosive materials required to manufacture gunpowder. During the First World War, the factory was very active but closed soon afterwards.

On the western side of the Errwood Reservoir lie the grounds and ruins of Errwood Hall, the former home of the Grimshawe family. Samuel Grimshawe, who built the hall in the early 1840s, came from a rich merchant family from Manchester.

The last of the Grimshawes died in 1930, and the hall was demolished when Fernilee Reservoir was built. Ruins of the hall still remain, the approach to which is particularly attractive when the rhododendron bushes that line the route are in bloom. The family cemetery can still be seen.

14. Wildboarclough (SK984687)

The tiny village of Wildboarclough, tucked away in a secluded picturesque valley between Leek and Congleton, off the A54, tends to get missed by visitors. This is a pity as it is in a beautiful setting, in the shadow of Shutlingsloe, Cheshire's 'Matterhorn', from the top of which on a clear day you get outstanding views over the Cheshire Plain and beyond.

Today, the parish is largely rural and sparsely populated, but it was once the home to several textile mills and the now peaceful valley hummed to the sound of clanking machinery. It made a significant contribution to the Industrial Revolution and 600 men were once employed here, and signs of the parish's industrial past are still visible today to the curious observer.

Crag Mill was built in 1793 for the spinning and printing of calico and other cloths. Designs were printed at the mill on plain carpets, one of which was exhibited at the Great Exhibition of 1851.

At one time there were three mills in the valley, but they were mostly demolished by 1957. Only a few outbuildings remain as well as the imposing three-storey administration office for Crag Mill, which at one time was used as a very grand village post office, probably the largest in any village in England. A little higher up the valley side is Crag Hall, built around 1800 by the then mill owner, George Palfreyman.

The attractive sixteenth-century church of St Saviour is an Edwardian Gothic red-sandstone building that stands in a slightly elevated position, which considering

Former Crag Mill Administration Centre, Wildboarclough.

Wildboarclough flood
marker, 1989.

the valley's propensity to flood is just as well. The most recent serious flood took place on 24 May 1989 when a tidal wave swept down Clough Brook, destroying several bridges and sections of road.

The Crag Inn was originally built in 1629 as a farm. It was converted to a beerhouse in 1825, and many of the traditional features still remain today. Blaze Farm and Tearooms, on the A54, where you can sample the famous Hilly Billy Ice Cream, which is made on the farm, is a little gem.

15. Flash Bar (SK032678)

For the tired walker having trekked across the wild windswept moorland and the cyclist toiled to the top of Axe Edge, Flash Bar must seem like an oasis with its smart welcoming café and pub. Situated just outside the village of Flash, on the A53, the stylish café and stores is possibly the highest shop and café in England. Opposite, the Traveller's Rest public house has now reopened as the Knight's Table.

Flash is surrounded by magnificent moorland scenery, stands at a height of over 1,500 feet above sea level and is claimed to be the highest village in England. It is an isolated place, the main part of which consists of well-weathered cottages and a small church, all clustered together seemingly to keep warm on the side of Oliver Hill, together with the New Inn.

On a sunny day when the sky is clear you can see for miles over the surrounding countryside, and as you walk across the moors, listening to the birds singing and keeping a watch out for wildlife, it is easy to imagine you are in paradise. At another time, on a different day, the picture may be quite the reverse, when the A53 is blocked by snow. It is often one of the first roads in the country to be closed after heavy snowfall.

Only a short distance from the village is Three Shires Head, where a bridge crosses the River Dane at a point where the borders of Derbyshire, Staffordshire and Cheshire meet. Many years ago illegal prizefights used to take place there, as the police were not allowed to cross county borders, so it was easy for the wrongdoers to flee into another county. For the very same reason, counterfeiters choose the spot for their unlawful trade – 'flash' is the name given to the illegal money. The word flash has since become associated with being dishonest, or for goods that are not of genuine quality.

Flash Bar Store
and Tearooms.

New Inn, Flash.

The village had its own benefit society to support those most in need, the Flash Loyal Union Society, established in 1846, nicknamed the 'Teapot Club', presumably because many members saved the money in a teapot. Attendance once a year at an annual feast was compulsory for members when the money was placed in the fund. Feast Day was an important day in the village's social calendar and when in 1995 the benefit club had to be disbanded due to new government regulations, the event was retained.

As one visitor who just happened to visit Flash on the day of the village parade recounts, she was astonished to see a procession march all the way to the Traveller's Rest carrying a large model teapot. Even more so as the marchers also carried banners referring to the teapot and were accompanied by a brass band. On the same day there is a service in the church and also a well dressing and flower festival takes place, and refreshments are provided in the village hall.

16. Solomon's Temple, Grin Low (SK056717)

Ascend the spiral staircase at Solomon's Temple, on Buxton's southern side, to enjoy some spectacular views across the High Peak. Looking beyond the impressive Dome of the former Devonshire Hospital, in fine weather you can see Mam Tor at Castleton on the horizon, and beyond that, Kinder Scout.

The two-storey folly is 20 feet high and sits on top of a ridge 1,440 feet above sea level. It was built in 1896 to replace an earlier building, requisitioned by Solomon Mycock, to give work to some of the unemployed in Buxton in the early nineteenth century. It occupies the site of an ancient burial mound, and during the construction work an archaeological dig revealed several Bronze Age skeletons from the Beaker period and later Roman artefacts.

Lower down the hillside, the 100-acre woodland was planted by the 6th Duke of Devonshire around 1820 to hide quarrying and limestone burning operations from the town. The old quarry is now occupied by Grin Low Caravan Club Site, where there are pitches for 150 touring caravans and tents. The woodland has now been designated a Site of Special Scientific Interest due to the wide range of plant life and the many wild animals and birds that frequent the woods.

Solomon's Temple, Grin Low, Buxton.

After enjoying the wonderful views and woodland walks you can visit Poole's Cavern show cave lower down the hillside, and take a guided tour of its magnificent underground chambers. Described by Charles Cotton in 1681 as 'The First Wonder of the Peak', the incredible stalactites, stalagmites and crystal flowstone have earned the show cave the title of the 'most spectacular cavern in Derbyshire'. Refreshment facilities and a car park are available. Go Ape is the latest attraction to be launched at Buxton Country Park. It uses the same car park as Poole's Cavern and is an award-winning high wire forest adventure course of rope bridges, Tarzan swings and zip slides, all set up in the treetops.

View of Buxton from Grin Low.

Poole's Cavern, Buxton.

17. 'Cathedral of the Peak' (Church of St John the Baptist), Tideswell (SK152757)

Tideswell is a large, very well-kept upland village of considerable character, ablaze with colour in the summer, with hanging baskets and flower tubs everywhere. Its church, dedicated to St John the Baptist, with its superb pinnacled tower, has dominated the village for over 600 years and is referred to as the 'Cathedral of the Peak'.

The rebuilding of the church started in 1346 and it was fifty years later before it was finally completed. The Black Death that swept the country interrupted work for a lengthy period in the early stages. Inside, the church is spacious and lofty, with many fine carvings, brass and stained-glass windows. A good number of the carvings are the work of Advent Hunstone, who was encouraged by Canon Andrew, the vicar, to switch from the family stone masonry business to woodcarving. This he did to great effect and much of his and his family's work is seen in churches far beyond Derbyshire.

The popular television programme *Songs of Praise* visited Tideswell during October 2002, but it is for the singing exploits of Singer Slack that the village is best known. Samuel Slack, born in 1757, was a noted bass singer. He was commanded to

St John's Church, Tideswell.

The George Hotel
adjoining Tideswell
Church.

sing before George III, and as a young man he competed for a place in the College
Choir at Cambridge. After he had sung, there was a stunned silence and none of the
other contestants took the opportunity to sing after such an awesome performance.
Such was the high opinion of Singer Slack that he was invited to lead the choir in
Westminster Abbey. He declined, preferring to sing with his friends in the village.

One interesting story of Slack's exploits tells the tale of how he lay down in a field
to recover from a slight overindulgence at the pub, only to be aroused by a snorting
bull. Restored to sobriety, he jumped up and gave such a loud bellow that the animal
took fright!

18. Litton Mill and Cressbrook Mill, Millers Dale (SK160729 and SK173728)

The scenery in Millers Dale, off the B6409, south of Tideswell, is magnificent, with
the impressive Ravenstor Cliff only a short distance down the road from the village of
Millers Dale, on the route to the once infamous Litton Mill. The richness of flora and
fauna along the dale sides has resulted in the area being designated a Site of Special
Scientific Interest and Derbyshire Wildlife Trust has several nature reserves in the area.

At the eastern end of the dale is Litton Mill, a small hamlet grouped around a former
cotton mill on the River Wye. The mill originally opened in 1782 and became notorious
for the inhuman behaviour of Elis Needham, the owner, towards his child labourers.

Many of the children were orphans, both local and from as far away as London.
The hours they had to work were long, the food was insufficient, the accommodation
cramped; beatings and general abuse by the owner of the mill and his family were
commonplace. Many died as a result of the harsh treatment they received.

Robert Blincoe was one boy who survived and he wrote a harrowing tale of the
cruelty and inhuman treatment handed out to the millworkers. It is said to have

helped promote the Factories Act of 1833 and may have even influenced Charles Dickens when he wrote *Oliver Twist*. The mill still remains, now converted into flats.

At Cressbrook Mill, around a mile to the east, William Newton, probably better known as the 'Minstrel of the Peak', was the manager of the mill and showed much greater compassion for his workers than that shown at Litton. He built a school and a row of latticed-windowed cottages that look down on the mill, now converted to luxury apartments.

Litton Mill.

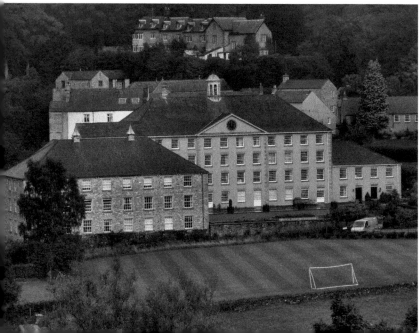

Cressbrook Mill.

19. Monsal Head, Monsal Dale (SK186215)

Monsal Head, on a minor road from Ashford in the Water, looks down on the dale below, from where you get a wonderful view of the Headstone Viaduct. Yet John Ruskin, the poet and conservationist, ranted when it was built: 'The valley is gone – and now every fool in Buxton can be in Bakewell in half an hour and every fool at Bakewell in Buxton.' Despite the initial controversy over the building of the viaduct in Monsal Dale, it is now considered an important feature of historic and architectural interest. When the railway line closed after 100 years and plans were mooted to demolish the viaduct, there was a widespread protest. The answer came in 1970, with the award of a preservation order.

It was in the 1860s that the London Midland Railway first ran over the viaduct, linking St Pancras and Manchester. The railway closed in 1968 and the line remained unused for twelve years before being taken over by the Peak District National Park.

The track has been converted into a route for walkers, cyclists and horse riders, known as the Monsal Trail. It runs for 8.5 miles from Coombs Road Viaduct, a mile south-east of Bakewell to the head of Chee Dale, around 3 miles east of Buxton. The route north from Monsal Head follows the deep limestone valley of the River Wye through breathtaking countryside.

Monsal Head Viaduct.

At the Monsal Head viewpoint, you can either relax on a seat or enjoy a walk. There are several footpaths down to the River Wye, which flows through the valley. All are quite steep, but you will be well rewarded for your effort and have the opportunity to walk across the viaduct and through the well-lit Headstone Tunnel. For refreshment, you can choose from the welcoming Hobbs Café or enjoy the comforts of Monsal Head Hotel.

20. Longnor's Historic Market Square (SK090649)

Set in lonely moorland countryside, 6 miles to the south-east of Buxton and close to the Derbyshire border, is the ancient village of Longnor. It has the appearance of a miniature town, complete with its own small market square, and attracts large numbers of visitors. They come to explore the upper reaches of the valleys of the River Dove and River Manifold and the rugged scenery that surrounds them.

Little was heard of Longnor, in what was a wild and desolate area at the northernmost boundary of Staffordshire, before the first written reference to the founding of St Bartholomew's Church in 1223. According to tradition, however, a church was built in the village around AD 700, following the formation of a Christian community.

In the early days agriculture was the main occupation of the few people who lived in the area, but by the mid-1600s there were four annual fairs and two weekly markets. The opportunities to trade had the effect of attracting more and more people to Longnor, and as a consequence its importance rapidly increased. Local farms provided food for the table and new trades sprang up. On market days the streets were thronging with people buying and selling goods and the pubs were busy with thirsty drinkers.

Longnor view.

Looking towards
Longnor
Marketplace.

The population continued to rise and by the mid-nineteenth century Longnor was referred to as a market town. It held its position as a small market town until the disappearance of the coaching age, when gradually easier access to other towns and cities improved and businesses moved away to Buxton and Leek. By the onset of the twentieth century, although agriculture still retained its importance, increasing mechanisation meant a smaller labour force was required, and workers migrated to newer industries. Despite losing its status as a market town, Longnor still has facilities that are the envy of many other villages.

Today, visitors arriving in Longnor, with its picturesque cobbled market square, enjoy exploring its little alleyways and visiting St Bartholomew's Church. A strange superstition existed at one time that it was considered bad luck if the church clock struck three during a funeral service, as it was said a further death would soon take place. So serious was this view taken that if a funeral service overran, the clock would be stopped.

Left: Longnor Craft Centre.

Below: The Cheshire Cheese, Longnor.

What most attracts the visitor's eye is the craft centre and coffee shop, housed in the handsome old market hall, a Grade II listed building dating back to 1873. At the time it was rebuilt at the direction of the Harpur-Crewe family, Longnor was a prosperous market town and it retains an inscription above the entrance giving the tariffs of long-forgotten market tolls.

21. The Magpie Mine, Sheldon (SK173682)

Lead mining is mentioned time and again in books on the Peak District. It seems entirely appropriate therefore to list the three most important places that you should visit to learn more about this fascinating subject. Those are the Peak District Mining Museum, housed in the Pavilion at Matlock Bath, the Temple Mine close to the museum and the Magpie Mine on the limestone uplands near Sheldon.

Standing one-third of a mile south of Sheldon, Magpie Mine can be seen silhouetted against the skyline from some distance away. It is around 1,050 feet above sea level with roads approaching it from Sheldon and Monyash. Members of the public may visit for external inspection at any reasonable time and whether you have any special interest in lead mining or not, you will find the site fascinating.

The mine has a recorded history from 1739, but dates back much further and is said locally to be well over 300 years old. Protracted troubles broke out in the 1820s and 1830s between the miners of Magpie, Maypitts and Red Soil mines. The dispute revolved around a vein of lead, and at various times the miners broke through into each other's workings. Often when this occurred, one side would light a fire underground and try to smoke the other out. Tragically, in 1833, three Red Soil miners were suffocated to death by a fire lit by the Magpie miners.

Following a year in prison and a lengthy court case at Derby Assizes, five Magpie miners were acquitted of the charge of murder owing to conflicting evidence and the lack of intent. The three widows of the Red Soil miners reputedly put a curse on the mine and supposedly a ghost was seen there in 1946.

Magpie Mine,
Sheldon.

In 1842, there were two deaths at the Magpie Mine and during the next fifty years the mine was dogged by problems caused by flooding and fire. In 1880, the company operating the mine even changed its name to the Magpie Mining Company, probably in the hope of ridding itself of the curse!

After a period of inactivity, several attempts were made to revive the mine, the last in the 1950s. However, in 1958, the constant battle with flooding and falling prices forced the closure of the mine. It is now a Scheduled Ancient Monument and is the most complete example of a lead mine remaining in the Peak District. There is quite a lot to see at the site, which is well served by public footpaths.

Further information regarding the mine may be obtained from the Peak District Mining Museum (telephone number: 01629 583834) or by visiting the website: www.peakdistrictleadminingmuseum.co.uk.

22. The High Peak Trail

The trail runs from High Peak Junction on the Cromford Canal to Dowlow, near Buxton. The original intention had been to construct a canal to connect William Jessop's Cromford Canal with Benjamin Outram's Peak Forest Canal. Difficulties, however, in ensuring an adequate water supply on the limestone moors led to the scheme being dropped.

Proposals were then put forward, and accepted, to build a railway, which was constructed on a similar alignment to the abandoned canal project. This involved steep inclines, up and down which wagons were hauled on cables by steam-driven winding engines.

The creation of the Cromford and High Peak Railway line was considered to be an engineering masterpiece and has attracted railway enthusiasts, not only from this country but all over the world. It linked High Peak Junction at 277 feet above sea level with Whaley Bridge at 517 feet. In the middle, it rose to over a 1,000 feet at Ladmanlow.

Ascending High Peak Trail from Cromford Canal.

Approaching Middleton Top along the High Peak Trail.

Stretching for 33 miles in length, the line was fully opened in 1831, when it was used to transport minerals, corn, coal and other commodities from one canal to the other.

Initially, horses were relied on to pull the trucks along the flatter parts of the route, but steam began to replace them in 1833 when the first locomotive came on the scene. However, it was some thirty years before horses were entirely replaced by locomotive power. The line continued to play an integral part in linking the canal system until 1853 when it was connected to the rapidly expanding railway network and became a branch line serving local needs.

At the eastern end of the trail is a catch pit, built following an accident in 1888 in which two wagons jumped across both the canal and the Midland Railway! The last accident occurred in the 1950s and the wreckage still remains.

Following the closure of the Cromford and High Peak Railway, it was purchased jointly by Derbyshire County Council and the Peak Park Planning Board, and in partnership with the Countryside Commission was converted into the High Peak Trail. Having been in existence for a number of years, the trail now forms a wonderful habitat for wildlife and is popular with all ages. It provides the disabled and less fit with an opportunity to enjoy the countryside along the flatter sections.

23. Hartington Cheese Shop (SK128604)

The picturesque village of Hartington is on the B5054 around 2 miles to the west of the A515 Ashbourne to Buxton road. Its spacious marketplace, village green, delightful duck pond and limestone houses, which sparkle in the bright sunlight, make it one of the major tourist centres in the Peak District. It has the air of a prosperous market town more than a village.

Apart from tourism, Hartington's main industry was cheese making, until the factory closed in May 2009. The original factory, opened in the 1870s, was the only survivor of seven that at one time operated in the area. It closed after around twenty years, but was soon returned to action and had the distinction of achieving a royal warrant to supply Stilton to George V in the 1920s and 1930s.

Above:
Village Stores,
Hartington.

Left: Old Cheese
Shop, Hartington.

Hartington village pump.

At its peak, the factory produced no less than a quarter of the world's supply of Stilton. Legally, the cheese can only be made in the three shire counties of Derby, Nottingham and Leicester – had the factory been built a quarter mile to the west it would not have qualified, being outside the county boundary in Staffordshire.

After the factory had been closed for three years, cheese-making production restarted in the parish. In October 2012, thanks to five individuals who were passionate about cheese making and keeping production in Hartington alive, a company called Hartington Creamery was set up and a number of barns in the parish were converted into small-scale cheese factories. The firm has recently received accreditation to make Stilton again.

The cheese shop has been established for thirty years, in a beautiful old stone building overlooking Hartington duck pond. It is hugely popular with local people and visitors alike, but if you cannot make it to the shop, you can still order online.

24. The Roaches (SK009615)

The Roaches – derived from the French *Les Roches*, meaning 'the rocks' – with Hen Cloud and Ramshaw Rocks form a gritstone escarpment off the A53 Leek to Buxton road. Here the rocks have been worn into unusual shapes by the elements and mark the south-western edge of the Peak District. On a clear day there are panoramic views from the rocks over much of Cheshire and even as far as Snowdon.

It is an area of rock and heather and belonged to the Swythamley estate prior to its break-up, following which it was purchased in 1980 by the Peak District National Park Authority. From May 2013, Staffordshire Wildlife Trust took on the management of the Roaches estate, which is enormously popular with walkers, climbers and wildlife enthusiasts.

Rock climbers on the Roaches.

Road to Roaches Hall.

Ramshaw Rocks, which rise impressively above the A53, have a rather unusual feature. As you approach the rocks from the Leek direction you will see, on your left, the rough outline of a man's head with a gap in the eye socket, which appears to wink at you as you pass. This is caused by rocks behind obscuring the sky for a moment. Not surprisingly, the rock formation is known as the Winking Man and a little further along the road towards Buxton is a pub of the same name.

The area was once famous for its wallabies. These were released during the Second World War from a private zoo at Swythamley and managed to breed and survive until the late 1990s, when the last survivors seemed to have disappeared; although there have been more recent claims made by visitors of having seen a wallaby when out walking.

Roaches Tearooms, Paddock Farm.

Along the road from Hulme End you will find Roaches Tearooms at Paddock Farm, which apart from good food has outstanding views over Tittesworth Reservoir towards Leek.

25. Meerbrook and Tittesworth Reservoir (SK989608)

Meerbrook, off the A53 Leek to Buxton road, is a small village on the south-western edge of the Peak District, set in a beautiful location, surrounded by some of the finest countryside that the Staffordshire Moorlands has to offer. The Roaches tower above the village and the attractions of Tittesworth Reservoir are to the south.

Part of the village was lost in the 1950s when the reservoir was constructed. Today, the area is popular with walkers, water sports enthusiasts and other outdoor fans as well as those who just want to sit and relax at the visitor centre or by the shoreline of the reservoir.

There was a settlement at Meerbrook as early as the thirteenth century and the Cistercian abbey of Dieulacres at Abbey Green, near Leek, had three granges in the area concentrating on sheep farming. Although predominantly a farming area, a coalfield covering an area of around 4 square miles, lying between Axe Edge and the Roaches, was developed from around the 1600s, until 1878. At nearby Upper Hulme there was a silk mill, which continued in operation until 1970.

Meerbrook provides a base for a wide variety of activities in addition to walking and climbing on the Roaches and those associated with Tittesworth Reservoir. The village school closed in 1969 and the building is now a youth hostel, and there is also a spacious modern village hall that is let out for a variety of leisure uses. An annual Scarecrow Festival is held each May.

There was a small church built at Meerbrook before the Dissolution of the Monasteries in 1538. The present parish church of St Matthew was erected in two phases in 1870 and 1873, where in June the Church Fête is held, in July the Flower Festival, and in November the Christmas Fair. Services are held fortnightly at the Methodist Chapel.

The Lazy Trout is a popular village pub, where you can dine both inside and out. The beautiful rear gardens have superb views of the Roaches.

Above: Tittesworth Reservoir.

Left: Lazy Trout, Meerbrook.

Eastern Peak District

26. Hathersage's Literary Connections (SK234818)

Charlotte Brontë is usually associated with the village of Haworth in Yorkshire, where the family moved in 1820 when she was four years of age. Her close friend at school was Ellen Nussey, whose brother was vicar of Hathersage. In 1845, Charlotte stayed at the vicarage with Ellen for around three weeks to prepare for the return of the vicar and his wife from honeymoon.

George Hotel, Hathersage.

It was from this visit to Hathersage that Charlotte drew the inspiration to write her most famous novel, *Jane Eyre*. Arriving by stagecoach, Charlotte was met at the George Inn by the landlord, Mr James Morton, whose surname she is accredited to have used for the fictitious village in her novel.

During her stay Charlotte took the opportunity to explore, walking on the moors and visiting many of the houses scattered around the area. Several of the places she saw on her walks have almost certainly been included in her book and, although renamed, can be identified from her descriptions.

Thornfield Hall, where Jane meets Rochester, fits the description of North Lees Hall. It was one of seven halls built around Hathersage by Robert Eyre for his seven sons. Visiting the church, Charlotte would have seen the Eyre brasses and have remembered the name.

In August 1847, the novel was published and copies sold very quickly, although not reviewed favourably by all critics. It obtained the royal seal of approval when Queen Victoria read extracts to Prince Albert. Even Charlotte's stern father was impressed and further editions were printed, from which Charlotte earned the substantial sum (in those days) of £500.

Charlotte married Arthur Bell Nicholls in 1854 at Haworth Church, but died the following year. However, her name and that of the Brontë family still lives on, with thousands of people every year visiting the Brontë Museum in Haworth. The popularity of her book *Jane Eyre* has never declined.

Another famous character associated with Hathersage is the outlaw Robin Hood, who is said to have been born at Loxley, only 8 miles from Hathersage, and many local places bear his name. His faithful lieutenant Little John is reputedly buried in Hathersage churchyard, in a grave measuring 11 feet from head to footstone.

The grave was opened in 1784 and a thigh bone 30 inches in length exhumed, which would make the occupant over 7 feet tall. For many years a great bow, arrows and a green cap hung in the church. In the porch is a large 600 year old stone said to have once marked Little John's grave.

Little John's Grave, St Michael's Churchyard, Hathersage.

View from
Hathersage
Church
steps.

27. David Mellor Cutlery Factory, Hathersage (SK233808)

Between Leadmill Bridge and Hathersage, off the B6001, is the Round Building, a purpose-built cutlery factory. It has been constructed out of what was once a gasworks, which will come as something of a surprise to the newcomer.

The factory has been described by Sir Michael Hopkins, one of the leading figures in the introduction of high-tech architecture into Britain as 'a minor masterpiece of modern architecture'.

Set discreetly back from the road, this highly functional industrial building hides its beauty away from the casual observer hurrying by along the busy road. It is only when it is approached up the gravel driveway and the whole site explored, that it is possible to fully appreciate the architectural value of the Round Building and the more recent additions.

The factory is internationally famous for its David Mellor cutlery, designed from the 1950s to the present day. A visit to the museum shows why he is often referred to as the 'Cutlery King'. The Design Museum may be visited during the week, where a wide range of designs is on display. There is also a country shop.

The café is equipped with all the finest David Mellor tableware and serves light lunches as well as specialist teas, coffees and cakes. It has its own traffic lights, which will astonish most first time visitors until they learn that David Mellor designed them in 1966 and that they are still in use today. He also designed a square pillar box for the Post Office, but this was not so successful.

Above: David Mellor factory, Hathersage.

Left: Exhibits outside David Mellor Museum.

28. Bole Hill Quarry, Grindleford (SK247792)

The opening of the Totley Tunnel signalled the arrival of the railway in the valley, which benefited the mineral extraction industry. The railway company used stone, but it most importantly provided an easy means of distribution to more distant places. All this activity brought prosperity to an area where the population grew rapidly.

Bole Hill Quarry.

Over a million tons of gritstone from Bole Hill was transported by train, for use in the construction of the Howden and Derwent Dams, which were built between 1901 and 1916. Royal assent for the reservoirs having been granted in 1899, a new railway infrastructure was constructed to assist in transportation to the site from Bamford.

Close by Bole Hill Quarry are stacks of abandoned cylindrical millstones lying on the ground, which make an impressive sight as they are gradually reclaimed by nature. The three main purposes that millstones served were for grinding grain into flour, grindstones for the cutlery trade and for pulping timber for paper production. Stones for the paper industry were exported all over the world between the 1890s and the 1950s, with a few still being exported as late as the 1970s.

The millstones have been abandoned as a result of faulty construction and because demand ceased and nobody wanted to take them away due to their great weight. They can be found alone or in small groups in various locations in the Peak District, most particularly near the two main centres of production above Hathersage and Grindleford. It is though not just walkers who happen to stumble across discarded millstones. They are the symbol of the Peak District National Park, and there is one by the roadside alongside every main road that enters the park.

To find Bole Hill from Surprise View car park, on the A6187, walk back along the footpath by the side of the road towards Hathersage, before turning left along a green trackway to reach your destination.

29. Padley Chapel (SK245794)

Padley Chapel lies along an access track a short distance from Grindleford Station, off the B6521 Grindleford to Longshaw road.

Grindleford Station Café is very popular with walkers and one of the busiest in the Peak District. Here groups of walkers can book early morning breakfasts at the

Padley Gorge, Grindleford.

weekend, before embarking on a voyage of exploration in the lovely countryside that surrounds Padley Gorge.

Although Padley Hall fell into ruins, Padley Chapel is hidden away on the upper floor of the gatehouse and still survives to this day. It served for many years as a farm building, before it was restored as a Roman Catholic chapel in 1933. It is thought to date back to the fourteenth and fifteenth centuries and came into the hands of Sir Thomas FitzHerbert following his marriage to Anne Eyre in the sixteenth century.

The FitzHerberts were staunch Roman Catholics and the hall was regularly raided to try to find evidence of Roman Catholic worship, until in July 1588 two Catholic priests were found, Nicholas Garlick and Robert Ludlam. They and several members of the FitzHerbert family were arrested.

It was not illegal to be a Catholic, but training abroad to be a priest was against the law. Harbouring a priest was a treasonable offence. Nicholas Garlick, the son of a yeoman from Glossop, who had trained to be a priest in France, and Robert Ludlam, the son of a farmer from Radbourne, who had also trained in France, were taken to Derby and hung, drawn and quartered. John FitzHerbert of Padley and his brother both died in prison.

An annual pilgrimage to Padley in honour of the martyrs began in 1898 and still takes place every year in July when a special service is held in the chapel in memory of the Padley martyrs.

Padley Chapel,
Grindleford.

30. Longshaw Estate (SK267801)

Longshaw estate is located in excellent walking country on the moors above Grindleford and is open to the public. Its dramatic location and topography attract many hundreds of thousands of visitors. Although seemingly remote it lies only a ten-minute drive from Sheffield.

The lodge at Longshaw was built around 1827 on the Duke of Rutland's estate to provide a retreat for his shooting guests, who included George V and the Duke of Wellington. It was purchased from the duke by public subscription in 1927 and presented to the National Trust.

In the outbuildings of Longshaw House the National Trust has established a visitor centre, where you can purchase gifts and take refreshment. The house was let for a while as a 'Holiday Fellowship' guest house, but was later converted into private apartments by the National Trust.

Longshaw House.

To the rear, by the large public car park, is the Moorland Discovery Centre, a lifelong learning centre aimed at encouraging groups of all ages to experience the wonderful moorlands of the Peak District National Park. At the front of the lodge is Longshaw Pasture.

The sheepdog trials held on Longshaw Pasture are of interest to both the country lover and city dweller, providing a wonderful spectacle for the visitor and local person alike. They are claimed to be the country's oldest trials for sheepdogs. The first official event took place on 24 March 1898 and they still take place annually, interrupted only by the two world wars. Eagerly awaited by enthusiasts, both local and national, they provide sporting entertainment and funds for charity.

After the Second World War in 1945, when the trials recommenced at Longshaw, the BBC was present to record the events. A popular long-running television series followed, bringing *One Man and his Dog* into the living rooms of millions of viewers.

31. Eyam – The Plague Village (SK218765)

Any tourist visiting the beautiful village of Eyam for the first time not knowing of its tragic history will rapidly become aware of it by reading the plaques on the walls of buildings. The people of this village once endured an epic struggle. In a period of just over twelve months, from September 1665, 260 people died from the plague out of a population of around 800. This has resulted in Eyam becoming one of the most visited villages in the Peak District, not just for its sheer beauty, but because visitors are curious about its tragic past.

The plague started when George Vicars, a tailor, was lodging in one of the cottages next to the church. A packet of cloth arrived, but as it was damp after its long journey from London, he spread it out in front of the fire to dry. This released fleas concealed in the parcel, which were carriers of bubonic plague germs. The death of George Vicars was sudden; others soon followed, and the villagers started to panic.

Eyam 'Plague Cottages'.

St Lawrence Church, Eyam.

The disease seemed to abate during the winter, only for the plague to intensify during the following spring. The rector of Eyam, William Mompesson, and his predecessor Revd Thomas Stanley persuaded the villagers to shut themselves off from the outside world to avoid the spread of the disease. Some refused and left the village.

Those that remained accepted strict quarantine arrangements to help prevent the spread of the disease. Neighbouring villages left provisions at agreed pick-up points. Mompesson closed the church and held open-air services in Cucklet Delph to reduce the chance of infection. When the plague finally was over, whole families had been wiped out. The disease had been contained within the agreed boundary set by the people of Eyam, but at a dreadful cost.

Eyam Hall.

From the early 1900s an annual Plague Commemoration service has been held on the last Sunday in August, and the following Saturday there is a carnival and sheep roast. In more recent years well dressings have also been held at the end of August, making this a very popular time for visitors.

Further information on the plague, the industrial development of the village and much more can be found at Eyam's excellent little museum. Eyam Hall is also well worth a visit.

32. Colditz Castle, Calver Mill (SK242746)

The scattered settlement, off the A623 Baslow to Stoney Middleton road, at what is now known as Calver, grew in importance following the construction of the first bridge in the fifteenth century. It replaced a ford and made crossing far less hazardous.

It was only after the first bridge had been built across the Derwent and lead mining had become popular that Calver began to take shape into the pretty village that it is today. In 1778, a small mill was built close to the new bridge and this was soon followed by the building of a much larger water-powered cotton mill. The second building was destroyed and replaced by the impressive seven-storey granite building that still remains today.

During the Second World War it was used by the Ministry of Supply, and later as a factory that manufactured stainless-steel products, before eventually closing and being converted into luxury apartments. Today, as you stand by Calver Bridge you can get a good view through the trees of the handsome old mill, with bracken-covered Froggatt Edge rising up in the background.

Calver Mill.

The Bridge Inn
by the River
Derwent.

The mill achieved national recognition shortly after the Second World War when it was featured as 'Colditz', the notorious German POW camp in a popular television series. During the series, the swastika flew high above the mill, but no one was fooled. This was not the case during the war itself, when lights were lit on the moors nearby, fooling the German bomber pilots into thinking that Sheffield lay below and releasing their loads harmlessly onto the moors.

The 'old' and the 'new' bridges can be viewed from the Bridge Inn, a small friendly pub with two bars and large garden running down to the River Derwent. Further up the road, the Derbyshire Craft Centre has on display a large selection of crafts, plus a wide range of books and gifts, and a café.

33. Baslow Curiosities (SK252725)

Baslow is a delightful little village situated in the Derwent Valley on the northern edge of the Chatsworth estate, which seems to have had more than its fair share of unusual happenings. All this adds to the charm of this special place that took an early liking to innovation.

Sebastian de Ferranti, who lived at Baslow Hall in the early twentieth century, was a 'do it yourself man' with a passion for electricity. He experimented with central heating and other electrical appliances in addition to fitting double-glazing. Sadly, his efforts at battery poultry farming had disastrous consequences: the chickens were electrocuted.

In 1862, Lieutenant Colonel E. M. Wrench took over a medical practice in Baslow. He was a surgeon who had served in the army in both Crimea and India and was a great patriot. In 1866, he built Wellington's monument on Baslow Edge and in Chatsworth Park he carved an inscription on the face of what is now known as Jubilee Rock to commemorate Queen Victoria's Golden Jubilee. The rock was previously known as the Elephant Stone. Queen Victoria would not have been amused.

St Anne's Church, Baslow.

Watchman's Hut, Old Bridge, Baslow.

Thatched cottages at Baslow.

St Anne's is both a beautiful and unusual church – one clock tower has Roman numerals and is dated 1759 and the other has 'Victoria 1897' on its face to mark Queen Victoria's Golden Jubilee. Inside the church by the door, in a glass case, is a dog whip, which in the seventeenth and eighteenth centuries was used by the official 'dog whipper' to keep stray dogs in order during the service. The whip has a thong 3 feet long, which is still in excellent condition and is bound around the handle with leather. Some historians also claim that it was used to maintain order among worshippers and to wake up those who snored during the service!

Nowadays, Baslow's Devonshire Bridge, built shortly after the First World War, carries most of the traffic across the River Derwent. However, it is the Old Bridge, close to the church and built in 1603, which attracts the most interest from visitors with its impressive stone arches. It is the only ancient bridge across the Derwent never to have been destroyed by floods.

It replaced a wooden bridge that all able-bodied men in the village were required to watch on a rota basis, to ensure the weight restrictions were not broken. Anyone caught breaking the rules was fined. The tiny watchman's hut still remains, no doubt reduced in size by the heightening of the road. At one time it offered a shelter of sorts to Mary Brady, a local beggar, who often slept rough inside.

Along the route to Chatsworth House is a row of thatched cottages, unusual in that thatch is seldom seen in the Peak District.

34. Chatsworth Park (SK258706)

Chatsworth is one of the Treasure Houses of England with fine furniture, sculpture, tapestry, paintings and other works of art. Set in beautiful surroundings in the heart of the Peak District National Park, it attracts admiring visitors from all over the world. The gardens can be visited separately to the house and extend to 105 acres with 5 miles of footpaths to explore. Apart from rare trees, shrubs, formal hedges, temples, sculptures old and new, streams and ponds it is probably the famous waterworks that most catch the eye.

In 1829, Joseph Paxton was made head forester. On his first day he arrived at Chatsworth at 4.30 a.m., having travelled from London to Chesterfield by the

Chatsworth House.

Comet coach. As no one was available to greet him, he explored the grounds and later set the men to work, before having breakfast with the housekeeper and her niece, with whom he fell in love and eventually married. All this before nine o'clock in the morning!

Paxton began the process of putting the estate woodlands back into shape after a long period of neglect. He planted the pinetum, a comprehensive collection of pines, many of them new to this country. Large trees were carefully moved from locations outside Chatsworth and planted in the grounds.

In 1835, he started work on an arboretum and seven years later he built rockwork on the hillside, with waterfalls and cascades. Paxton oversaw the replacement of the estate village of Edensor and constructed the Emperor Fountain. He also built a conservatory – known as the 'Great Conservatory' – and a lily house, specially designed for a giant lily with a design based on the leaves of the plant.

Today, the park is free to walk in, except when one of Chatsworth's annual prestigious events is being held. It is a great place to visit and a first-rate stress buster.

35. Stand Wood, Chatsworth Park (SK267702)

The B6012 winds its way through the parkland at Chatsworth and provides a magnificent view of the house. You look across the River Derwent to the west and south front, with Chatsworth's neat lawns sloping up the hillside to Stand Wood, which presents a superb backcloth.

Parts of the wood have probably been wooded since medieval times, but the trees now growing there are of more recent origin. The mature beech trees at the crest

View from Stand
Wood over
Edensor.

Above: Swiss Cottage, Stand Wood.

Left: Hunting Tower, Stand Wood.

of the hill are the oldest and date back to the late eighteenth century. In the 1830s, Joseph Paxton saw Stand Wood as an extension to the pleasure ground and as a result the wood was extensively ornamented.

Today, you can walk in Stand Wood free of charge, or take the easier option of enjoying a twenty-eight-seater trailer ride. There are two main trails through the wood, of which one is quite easy and the other rather steeper. Whichever you choose you will be able to see the Swiss Lake, on the northern shore of which is the eye-catching Swiss Cottage, built as a gamekeeper's cottage a few years after the lake. It was designed to attract attention and impress visitors using the scenic carriage route. A short distance away the Emperor Lake feeds the fountain of the same name in the gardens at Chatsworth House.

Most impressive of all is the Hunting Tower. Elizabethan in construction, it provides awe-inspiring views over Chatsworth estate. Many years ago it was used by the ladies of the house to view the hunt when it took place in the park below. The cannon at the base of the tower came from a ship that fought at the Battle of Trafalgar. In 2006 a small stone outbuilding at the foot of the tower was converted to provide additional accommodation for groups wishing to stay in the tower.

36. Edensor, Chatsworth Park (SK250698)

Every year visitors from all over the world pass through Chatsworth Park on their way to visit the house and gardens or to just admire the view. Most only cast a cursory glance over towards the gateway that leads to Edensor, one of the most admired estate villages in the country. It is quite unique in style and provides the first time visitor with an experience they will never forget. Set in a walled enclosure within attractive parkland owned by the Devonshire family, with its fine buildings and majestic looking church the village just waits to be explored.

Originally, Edensor lay between the river and the road through the park, when the houses were set out in a straggling line down to the Derwent. This did not appeal to the 4th Duke of Devonshire, who spent considerable money and effort improving Chatsworth House, redesigning the gardens and building a grand new bridge over the river. He decided to demolish the houses visible from his home and rehouse the tenants in the nearby estate villages of Pilsley and Beeley. The duke died in 1764 prior to the completion of the work and it was the 6th Duke who completed the building of the present village.

Joseph Paxton, who remodelled and landscaped the gardens at Chatsworth, chose the site for the new 'Model Village', but it was John Robertson, a relatively unknown architectural assistant from Derby, who provided the designs. At that time aspiring young architects such as Robertson would prepare a book of house plans as part of their training.

It is thought that Robertson approached the duke to show him the plans when he was busy with other matters. After quickly looking through them he could not

Above: Looking down towards Edensor.

Left: House at Edensor.

make up his mind and chose all the different styles in the book, which proved to be a masterstroke. The designs ranged from Norman to Jacobean, and Swiss- to Italian-style villas. A few of the old houses that were well out of sight of Chatsworth House were left virtually untouched.

Robertson retained the fourteenth-century church, but it only remained for around thirty years after the completion of the village before it was replaced by a much larger one, built by George Gilbert Scott. The new church with its graceful spire and spacious layout added to the status and importance of the village, which its predecessor had failed to do.

37. Bakewell (SK218685)

When, in 1951, the Peak was the first of the national parks to be set up in England and Wales, Bakewell – the only sizeable market town in the park – was the logical choice as the administrative centre. From its offices at Aldern House, it controls an area of 542 square miles and covers parts of Staffordshire, Cheshire, Yorkshire and Greater Manchester as well as Derbyshire. The population, when the park was set up, was only 38,000 and has not changed much since that day.

The picturesque old market town of Bakewell is set in an excellent location on the banks of the River Wye, in the heart of the Peak District. At the weekend in winter, on Monday market days and during the summer it throngs with visitors who come to visit the famous Bakewell Pudding Shop, browse around its many shops and to enjoy refreshment at one of the numerous restaurants, pubs and cafés in the town. Others just enjoy a stroll around this historic little town with its fine old buildings and lovely river walks.

The five-arched bridge across the River Wye is one of the best-known landmarks in the Peak. It dates from 1200, is among the oldest in the country, and is now designated as an Ancient Monument. From here, you have the choice of two short river walks. The first is to go upstream through meadowland known as Scots Garden, passing Holme Hall, a small Jacobean manor built in 1626. Then cross the packhorse bridge, which is by the side of the sheep dip. The bridge was frequently used by

Wye Bridge, Bakewell.

Old Bakewell
Pudding Shop.

Bakewell
Museum.

packhorse leaders arriving from the Monyash direction, thus avoiding paying tolls in the centre of the town. Alternatively, you can walk southwards along the banks of the River Wye, where rainbow trout wait to be fed, down to the impressive-looking sports ground and then retrace your steps.

Bakewell's Olde House Museum is well worth seeking out, hidden away as it is behind the church. Originally a parsonage, it was later converted into six cottages by Sir Richard Arkwright; another four cottages were accommodated in the adjacent barn to house his workers at Lumford Mill. It is now one of the best-preserved fifteenth-century houses in the country, but only fifty years ago it was nearly demolished after the local council served a demolition order. There was a local outcry and the house was eventually saved and restored to its former glory by the Bakewell Historical Society.

Across from Rutland Square, at the far end of Bath Gardens, is the Bath House. Here the Duke of Rutland, who owned the premises, tried to establish a spa similar to those at Buxton and Matlock. The 'warm' water from the natural spring, at only 15 degrees centigrade, was much colder than that of its rivals, and the venture failed.

38. The River Derwent

The River Derwent has a truly remarkable tale to tell. Although only 60 miles in length, it fills mighty reservoirs near its source and has been harnessed to power mills and, most important of all, played an outstanding part in the Industrial Revolution. On its journey, it flows through parkland past Chatsworth, and later through the narrow gorge at Matlock, before continuing through meadows and the busy city of Derby on its way to a meeting with the River Trent.

Rising in the far north of Derbyshire, near the Yorkshire border, at Swains Greave between Bleaklow and Howden Moors, the River Derwent never leaves the borders of the county for its full course. It finishes its journey at Derwent Mouth, where it joins the River Trent, near the Leicestershire and Nottinghamshire borders.

For all the early part of its journey, the Derwent flows through the national park. Despite its modest length, the Derwent follows a course through a valley of contrasting landscapes. Wildly beautiful in the north, with majestic man-made dams and reservoirs, it is an area often referred to as the Peak District National Park's own

River Derwent stepping stones near Hathersage.

Above: River Derwent at Matlock Bath.

Below: River Derwent at Belper.

'Lake District'. Further south, as you enter Chatsworth Park, the terrain becomes much more soft and gentle.

Although the southern half of the valley is outside the Peak District National Park boundary, visitors are gradually discovering that the area has just as much to offer.

For hundreds of years the waters from the river were harnessed to turn grindstones in corn mills and to power hammers for the fulling of cloth and forging of metal. The waters also operated bellows to blast air into furnaces and to drive the frames and mules for spinning cotton. It was Richard Arkwright, later Sir Richard, who was the driving force behind the Industrial Revolution. He exploited water power to drive his machinery when he moved to Cromford and he is often referred to as the 'Father of the Industrial Revolution'. Further south at Belper, the visitor centre tells the story of Jedediah Strutt and his family who also played a major part in the Industrial Revolution. At Darley Abbey, it was the Evans family who contributed substantially to the story, and at Derby the Lombes. All this is set in an area of considerable scenic beauty.

Frequently referred to as the 'Cradle of the Factory System', the importance of Cromford and the Derwent Valley was recognised in 2001, when it was awarded World Heritage Status. The site extends from Masson Mill at Matlock Bath to the former Derby Silk Mill, a distance of approximately 15 miles, and is currently the only World Heritage Site in the East Midlands.

There can be no doubt that the Derwent Valley is one of the country's finest assets, both from the point of view of its heritage and magnificent scenery.

39. Stanton Moor (SK245635)

Set roughly between Stanton-in-Peak and Birchover is Stanton Moor, which rises to 1,096 feet above sea level and offers genuine moorland terrain. It is an isolated gritstone outcrop in the heart of limestone country and one of the richest prehistoric sites in Derbyshire. Although it is relatively small in size, it has a feeling of isolation despite its close proximity to neighbouring villages.

On the edge of the moor there are superb views of the surrounding countryside and, on the bracken-clad moor, several impressive boulders and reminders of the past. It is easy to reach from the Birchover to Stanton road and provides good level walking and is something of a 'hotspot' for walkers.

Last century, the Heathcote family father and son exhumed in excess of seventy burial mounds on the moor. Both were noted amateur antiquarians and between them they excavated the tumuli on Stanton Moor and built up a fascinating private museum in the old village post office at Birchover. When Percy Heathcote died the collection was transferred to Sheffield West Park Museum.

The most famous of the Bronze Age relics on the moor are the Nine Ladies Stone Circle. The circle was probably the scene of Bronze Age ceremonies dating back to around 1500 BC. Its name is based on the legend that nine ladies danced here on the sabbath and were turned to stone as a punishment, along with the fiddler who stands nearby.

Left: Cork Stone, Stanton Moor.

Below: Nine Ladies stone circle, Stanton Moor.

Stone quarrying has been an important industry in the area over a long period and provided employment for many local people. The whole subject of quarrying in such a beautiful area has been a very contentious subject for a number of years.

40. Caudwell's Mill and Peak Village Shopping Centre, Rowsley (SK256658 and SK258661)

Caudwell's Mill at Rowsley, off the A6 south of Bakewell, is a Grade II listed building set in a beautiful location close by the River Wye. A mill has stood in the village since at least the sixteenth century. The latest mill was built in 1874 by John Caudwell and run as a family business for over a century. When it closed, a group of enthusiasts got together to form a charitable trust to save what was the only complete Victorian water turbine – powered roller mill in the country.

They had a fight on their hands, as according to the Millers' Manual Association, milling machinery no longer needed must be destroyed to prevent reuse. After a lot of persuasive talk, an agreement was reached to waive the ancient right and allow a small amount of flour to be produced and the mill used for exhibition purposes.

The mill is a fine example of a working nineteenth-century mill, with water turbines powering the machinery. It was originally powered by two waterwheels, which drove eight pairs of millstones in the flour mill. The millstones were replaced over a century ago with roller mills.

Today, everything is in working order and the mill covers four floors and usually runs daily, although flour is no longer milled on the premises. There are several

Caudwell's Mill, Rowsley.

Paxton's station that never was at Rowsley.

displays, information panels and hands-on models throughout the mill to make your visit enjoyable and informative. The mill is normally open to visitors on a daily basis for a small charge. There is also a shop on the ground floor where a range of flours for baking may be purchased.

In addition, there is a busy craft centre on the site, with a well-stocked shop and a number of artisans' workshops and exhibition areas. The excellent café was constructed using wood from an old Scottish corn mill; the seating, tables and counter were salvaged from Crich Carr Chapel when it closed.

The Peak District's first and only Factory Outlet Shopping Centre at Rowsley occupies the site of a former railway marshalling yard. The centrepiece of which is Paxton's splendid station, which was left unused when the Duke of Devonshire was adamant that he would not allow the line across Chatsworth Park.

Southern Peak District

41. Thor's Cave, Manifold Valley (SK099551)

Thor's Cave is located between Weag's Bridge and Wetton Mill in the beautiful Manifold Valley, along the former Leek and Manifold Light Railway that has been converted into a trail for walkers and cyclists. The cave is one of Staffordshire's most important viewpoints, clearly visible for several miles away and from neighbouring roads that run through the valley. It is set in a rock face that rises steeply 350 feet above the Manifold Valley – an eerie, awesome and spectacular sight.

Thor's Cave,
Manifold Valley.

The cave's 60-foot entrance is very imposing, but inside it is comparatively small. A footbridge and a steep-stepped and sometimes slippery climb take you up to the cave from the valley floor. If you can make it you will be well rewarded for your effort by the excellent view. Lower down the cliff are a number of small caves just above water level.

Samuel Carrington, the Wetton schoolmaster, excavated the cave in the nineteenth century when he discovered many relics of prehistoric man. In all, excavations at the cave have revealed 10,000 years of remains, which make it one of the oldest inhabited sites in the Peak District. In addition, evidence has been found of Roman and Saxon occupation in more recent times. Some of the finds are on exhibition at Buxton Museum.

The area around the cave is used by rock climbers, some of the climbs being officially rated as very severe and only suitable for the experienced climber. The cave has been used as the location for several films, including the 1988 film *The Lair of the White Worm* directed by Ken Russell and starring Hugh Grant. It also appeared on the front cover of the Verve's debut album, *A Storm in Heaven*.

42. Wetton Mill (SK017561)

Wetton Mill, owned by the National Trust, is a very popular spot with visitors to the Manifold Valley, which lies a short distance to the north-west of Wetton.

It was originally a water mill for grinding corn, but closed in 1857. Situated by the side of the Manifold Way, it has now been converted to create a beautiful picnic spot, café and two National Trust holiday cottages. There are still some remnants of the old mill to be seen, with a few old limestone buildings, a section of the mill pond now impounded by the river, the millstream and a grindstone. The bridge that gives access to the mill yard was built by the 5th Duke of Devonshire in 1805.

The tearoom, housed in one of the former grist buildings at the mill, provides welcome refreshment to visitors who come to walk in the valley or just want to relax and admire the superb countryside. The valley has some of the most spectacular scenery in the Peak District and is rich with wildflowers, butterflies and birds.

The Leek and Manifold Light Railway used to run through the valley. Lack of sufficient business forced the early closure of the line and it has subsequently been turned into a trail for walkers and cyclists, only 2 miles of which is not car-free. In total, the trail runs for 9 miles from Hulme End Visitor Centre to Waterhouses Old Station car park.

Surprisingly, the riverbeds of the Manifold and Hamps that flow through the valley are frequently dry, as the waters soak away into the porous limestone rocks below and only reappear in wet weather. During dry weather, the Manifold disappears at Wetton Mill and re-emerges from its underground journey from a boil hole at Ilam.

Wetton is a compact little village of limestone cottages that seem to huddle together in an exposed position against the cold at an altitude of around 1,000 feet. Winters are now much milder, but some of the older residents still recall the times the village has been cut off from the outside world.

Above: Walkers at Wetton Mill.

Right: Wetton Mill Café.

Swainsley Tunnel,
Manifold Valley
Way.

43. Ilam Park (SK128508)

Alpine-style cottages, a Tudor Gothic hall, an eccentric river and a wonderful background of soft green hills make Ilam a very popular place. Many visitors come to walk in Ilam Hall's beautiful parkland along the aptly named Paradise Walk, which is fringed by woodland, planted as a pleasure ground for the hall.

It was here that Jesse Watts-Russell, a wealthy industrialist, had a rather grand hall built. It had battlemented towers, ornamental chimneys and a flag tower. The architect who designed the hall was also engaged in the building of Alton Towers, and there were some similarities between the two.

Following Watts-Russell's death, the hall was in the hands of the Hanbury family for a time before being tried unsuccessfully as a restaurant, then sold and partly demolished. In 1934, Sir Robert MacDougal was persuaded to buy it for the nation and give it to the Youth Hostels Association 'for the perpetual use of the youth of the world'.

As the YHA did not have a trust body, it gave the building to the National Trust. What remains today are the old entrance hall, armoury and servants' quarters, which have been converted into a youth hostel. There are tea rooms, a shop, information facilities and a car park available, free to National Trust members.

A short distance from the YHA is St Bertram's Bridge, which carried the old road across the River Manifold before the present road bridge existed. Bertram, who had connections with the royal family of Mercia, was returning from Ireland with his wife and newborn child. He left them briefly, only to find on his return that wolves had savaged them both. At once he denounced his heritage and spent the rest of his life as a hermit preaching the gospel.

In the Church of the Holy Cross, the chapel of St Bertram contains a shrine that became a place of pilgrimage in the Middle Ages and the scene of many miraculous cures.

Above: Ilam Hall.

Below: Cottages at Ilam.

44. Dovedale (SK152514)

The River Dove rises on high ground at Axe Edge, near to Buxton. Its clear waters meander southwards for 45 miles to eventually join the River Trent. For much of its course the river runs through stunningly attractive countryside, with one bank in Derbyshire and the other in Staffordshire. It is a walker's paradise, providing both easy walks for the casual walker as well as more strenuous hikes for the more energetic practitioner, with its steep-sided limestone sides and tree-covered slopes.

Along the stretch of the valley that runs from the tiny hamlet of Milldale, down to the large car park close to the road linking Ilam and Thorpe, the water has eroded the limestone into some spectacular rock formations. Examples of which are the Lion's Head and the natural archway in front of Reynard's Cave.

The building of the Midland Railway in 1863 made the Peak only three hours from London. Many were the thousands who got off the train at Alsop-en-le-Dale station and walked the length of Dovedale before catching a train home at Thorpe station. The railway is no more, but cars still bring thousands of visitors to what is one of England's most famous beauty spots.

Visitors to Dovedale on a busy day.

Dovedale stepping stones.

Photographs of the stepping stones across the Dove must have appeared on more calendars and gift boxes of all shapes and sizes than any almost any other countryside scene in England. The stones are quite stable and people of all ages love to cross them, although after heavy rain they can become submerged in the river.

The valley has been inhabited since the Ice Age, around 14,000 years ago, when hunters used the caves for shelter. Reynard's cave was used by early farmers to bury their dead, and at a later date, during the Roman occupation of the country, the caves provided shelter for shepherds tending their flocks.

45. Milldale (SK139548)

Milldale is a delightfully positioned hamlet at the northern end of Dovedale. It attracts walkers like few other places of its size in Britain. Most come to explore the beautiful Dove Valley, with its steep-sided limestone sides and tree-covered slopes.

The hamlet derives its name from an old mill and records show that there was a mill to the north of Viator's Bridge in 1775. The mill ceased to operate in the late 1870s and all that remains are the buildings to the left of the former mill. These have been converted into a National Trust Information Barn.

The mill processed and crushed calamine, mined at Chrome Hill and Parkhouse Hill, near Glutton, south of Buxton. Drug firms used the higher-quality calamine and lower grades were used in brass making. In the nineteenth century the mill was utilised to grind colours for paints. The remaining millstone wheel is still to be seen lying in the water by the riverbank.

Viator's Bridge, an ancient packhorse crossing over the River Dove at Milldale, is probably the most renowned of all the footbridges in the Peak District. It was made famous in the English classic *The Compleat Angler* by Izaak Walton. In the fifth edition, published in 1676, Charles Cotton of nearby Beresford Hall wrote an addendum about fishing, introducing the reader to two travellers – Charles Cotton (Piscator) and Izaak Walton (Viator).

In the days when the two travellers would have approached the narrow bridge, it would not have had any walls and must have looked quite frightening to cross. Bridges were then designed with low parapets to allow horses carrying panniers to cross without obstruction. Viator commented on seeing the bridge: 'Why! A mouse can hardly go over it: 'tis not twelve fingers broad.'

Today, Milldale consists of only a dozen or so cottages, the oldest of which date back to the seventeenth century, and the others probably the eighteenth century. There is no public house in the village, but only a short distance away at Hopedale is the Watts Russell Inn. Welcome refreshments can be obtained from a small shop window at Polly's Cottage at Milldale, named after a former occupant.

Millstone wheel from former mill at Milldale.

Above: Viator's Bridge, Milldale.

Below: Looking down Millway to Milldale.

46. Tissington Hall (SK174525)

Tissington, off the A515 from Ashbourne (3.5 miles) to Buxton road, is one of the prettiest and most unspoilt villages in the country. A sense of something rather special fills the minds of visitors when entering Tissington. First, you pass through large rusticated lodge gates and then along an avenue of 200-year-old lime trees. Surprisingly, the village is reached before the hall, with its pretty limestone cottages and well-tended gardens behind wide grass verges and backed by mature trees. Most of Tissington has been rebuilt, between 1830 and 1860, in traditional local style.

Further up the main village road is Tissington Hall, a fine Jacobean manor house, standing in a slightly elevated position above the road behind a walled garden. The wall is broken only by a handsome seventeenth-century gateway with wrought-iron gates by the famous Derbyshire blacksmith Robert Bakewell. The house was built in 1609 by Francis FitzHerbert, but has been much extended by his descendants. It replaced an earlier hall that stood on the opposite side of the road within the confines of an ancient Derbyshire hill fort.

Driveway to Tissington Hall.

Tissington Hall from Hall Well.

Today the hall is occupied by Sir Richard FitzHerbert, the 9th Baronet, and Lady Caroline FitzHerbert and their children. The FitzHerberts have owned the estate for over 500 years, but have managed to retain the village's quiet dignity and charm, while at the same time ensuring modern-day needs have been met in full. Well before the FitzHerbert family came to Tissington there is evidence of occupation from excavations in the area. Bronze Age, Anglo-Saxon and Celtic remains having all been discovered.

For those people who have not been on one of the popular escorted tours of the hall, their most lasting impression probably is the impressively long façade of Tissington Hall and its outbuildings. It fits into the surroundings perfectly, creating a feeling of importance and grandeur but without imposing itself too much on the exquisite village scene.

Major changes were made to the house in 1900 when a library and billiard room were added. During the general restoration work, the custom of the day of using plasterwork for wall decoration was used and it was discovered that twenty rooms had original Jacobean panelling. The restored oak panelling is now one of the most attractive features that visitors to the hall admire, with the ornately carved staircase particularly catching the eye. The very attractive gardens laid out by William Barron and Sons in 1913 open out into terraces and provide attractive views in all directions.

47. Parwich (SK187544)

Apart from walkers who come to explore the network of footpaths that pass through Parwich, situated between the A515 Ashbourne to Buxton road and the B5056, not many visitors to Derbyshire discover one of the prettiest villages in the county or have even heard of its existence. This changed somewhat though when the *Sunday Times*, in March 2015, nominated the village as 'one of the best places to live in Britain'.

On the edge of the Peak District, Parwich is not on any of the main routes through the area and as a result does not suffer from excessive traffic noise, as do so many other villages. Neat limestone houses of various shapes and sizes stand in picture postcard fashion along winding lanes and narrow ginnels. In the summer, the cottages with their attractive gardens, window boxes and hanging baskets provide a vivid splash of colour against the green background of the steeply rising hillside.

The hills rise above Parwich to over 1,000 feet, forming a rough uneven plateau where a considerable number of prehistoric remains have been found. There is evidence of some medieval lead mining in the locality, but the village was spared the worst ravages of the lead-mining boom. Farming has been very important to the village's prosperity, but it is now in decline and those people of working age mainly travel to other locations.

Cottages at Parwich.

Above: St Peter's Church, Parwich.

Below: Sycamore Inn, Parwich.

Attractive Parwich Hall, three storeys high, overlooks the village from its dominant position on the hillside. It has a mainly brick façade, which is rather unusual in this part of the Peak District, stone being less expensive. During the nineteenth century it was used as a vicarage, but the vicar was so unpopular with his parishioners that when he moved away they burned an effigy of him on the village green. It is now in private occupation.

The Sycamore Inn dates back to the seventeenth century, and the brick extension at the rear two centuries later. Here you can not only enjoy quality refreshment at this award-winning pub – it won the CAMRA 'Country Pub of the Year' award in 2015 – but also take home a bag of shopping. The pub has taken over from the last village shop, which closed a few years ago.

48. Roystone Grange, Pikehall (SK201568)

The easiest way to visit Roystone Grange is to park at the Minninglow car park by the High Peak Trail. This is around half a mile south of Pikehall on the Parwich road, off the A5012 Newhaven to Cromford road. Roystone Grange is a short distance south of the car park and can be approached using the trail and footpaths through the fields. There is a useful information board on site when you get there, but the appropriate Ordnance Survey map will help you choose the best route for your destination.

It was the arrival of steam trains that transformed this remote but stunningly attractive area, with the Cromford and High Peak Railway passing close to Pikehall. The track has now been converted into the High Peak Trail.

During Roman times a small native settlement was built near the present Roystone Grange Farm. It may have started as just one farmstead before the site was developed more extensively. A dig by Sheffield University discovered that the dry valley had been in continuous use since Roman times. The foundations of medieval Roystone Grange were also discovered. Some of the drystone walls still in use today were laid by the Romans.

Roystone Grange was a monastic sheep farm established by the Cistercian Garendon Abbey in Leicestershire. It was built in the twelfth century, but the abbey ceased farming around the late fourteenth century and it was leased to tenants. Today, turf-covered walls are all that survives.

The chapel-like structure on-site was in fact built in the nineteenth century as a pump house where a large water-cooled engine pumped compressed air through cast-iron pipes to drive the drills of the rock quarries in the valley. Two brick kilns can still be seen by the side of the former railway line, which was used to transport the finished bricks.

If you require refreshment after your exertions, the seventeenth-century inn Jug and Glass might meet your requirements. From Pikehall follow the A5012 to Newhaven, turn right along the A515, and the inn is on the left after around a mile.

Above: Footpath down to Roystone Grange.

Below: Roystone Grange farmhouse.

49. National Stone Centre, Wirksworth (SK284552)

The National Stone Centre, off the B5035 Cromford to Carsington road, occupies an area of disused quarries overlooking Wirksworth and crossed by the High Peak Trail. It sounds incredible, but every year each of us uses 5 tons of stone, which finds its way into an enormous number of products.

Derbyshire is the largest quarrying area in the country, and in the 1990s it produced 20 million tons of stone a year. This made the county an ideal site for the National Stone Centre, an educational charity supported by over eighty public, industrial and academic organisations.

It was officially opened in October 1990 on the site of six disused quarries, abandoned in the mid-1960s after providing stone for the M1. The exhibition at the visitor centre, reveals an extraordinary number of interesting facts about stone and the events that have affected our daily lives. There is also a gems shop and large café.

Outside the visitor centre, the quarry trail takes you back over 300 million years. Viewpoint panels along the trail indicate where you are: the bottom of a lagoon, the

View from National Stone Centre towards the High Peak Trail.

'Become a rock detective' at the National Stone Centre.

side of a reef, or by the tropical Derbyshire coastline! There are plenty of remains of animal life to be seen, with shellfish embedded in the rocks, and for the observant, sharks' teeth. Evidence of lead miners' pick marks can also be found.

The Millennium Wall at the centre was built by members of the Drystone Walling Association of Great Britain over a weekend in 2000. Wallers, both professional and amateur, travelled from all parts of the country to participate. There was even one who travelled over 1,100 miles from Orkney, just to act as a helper.

50. Wirksworth Barmote Court (SK288542)

The presence of lead brought prosperity to many towns and villages in and around the Peak District, and during the period between 1600 and 1780 lead mining was at its peak. As it became less economical because of international competition and extraction difficulties, mining started declining during the nineteenth century.

In 1288, the Inquisition for the King's Field of the High Peak held at Ashbourne gave the lead miner legal backing to the many customs and privileges that already existed in order to encourage mining in what was mainly a barren wasteland. Barmote Courts administered the laws and were presided over by barmasters. It is almost certainly the oldest industrial court in Britain, and possibly in the world.

Moot Hall, Chapel Lane, Wirksworth.

When a vein of lead had been discovered it had to be freed by giving a dish of ore to the barmaster and applying for the title to be registered. Having been granted possession of his mine, the first requirement for the miner was to erect a stowe (windlass) to signify ownership. If the mine was not worked for three weeks, except for flooding and ventilation problems, the barmaster would cut a notch or 'nick' in the stowe. This procedure would be repeated, usually at three-weekly intervals, and if after the third 'nicking' the mine was still unworked, ownership was forfeited and the stowe thrown down.

In the middle of the seventeenth century, Edward Manlove, a steward at the Barmote Court in Wirksworth, wrote a poem to assist miners in remembering the laws. The theft of ore was considered a very serious offence and the law was recorded as follows:

> For stealing ore twice from the minery,
> The thief that's taken fined twice shall be,
> But the third time that he commits such theft,
> Shall have a knife stuck through his hand to th'haft,
> Into the stow, and there till death shall stand,
> Or loose himself by cutting loose his hand,
> And shall forswear the franchise of the mine,
> And always lose his freedom from that time.

Originally there were two Barmote Courts, one at Monyash covering the High Peak and the other at Wirksworth, the Low Peak. In 1814, the Monyash court moved to Wirksworth, and since 1994 the two have met together, once a year, in April, at the Moot Hall in Chapel Lane, Wirksworth. In line with tradition, bread, cheese, clay pipes and tobacco are provided at the meetings.

Wirksworth itself does not perhaps make much impact on the busy traveller driving through. All those visitors, however, with time to explore the narrow streets and maze of interesting alleyways, to admire the old buildings and lovely views, to visit the ancient church and the cathedral-like close, will soon find themselves falling in love with this fascinating old town.

View over Wirksworth.

About the Author

Denis Eardley has been writing local interest features and walks for the *Derby Telegraph* for twenty years. He has compiled eleven Discover Derbyshire and two Discover Derby supplements, as well as writing for *Yesterday Today* and the award-winning *Derbyshire Magazine*. Denis also supplies the *Derby Telegraph* with weekly town and village profiles as well as walks, which are published during the spring and summer each year.

Denis lives in Derby and enjoys sport, photography and visiting towns, villages and the countryside in the UK with his family, which now includes two grandsons. He has written six books: *Around Wirksworth, Wirksworth and the Surrounding Area, Villages of the Peak District, Derwent Valley Walks – Derwent Valley Mills World Heritage, Picture the Past Derby* and *Derby From Old Photographs*.

Acknowledgements

Several people have assisted me in my research and presentation of this book. I would particularly like to thank Gillian Eardley and John Hollinshead for their help and support.